12 WOMEN IN MEDICINE

by Marne Ventura

12 STORY LIBRARY
MORE TO EXPLORE

www.12StoryLibrary.com

12-Story Library is an imprint of Bookstaves.

Photographs ©: Mary Noble Ours/NIDA(NIH)/PD, cover, 1; ZUMA Press, Inc./Alamy, 4; National Institutes of Health/PD, 5; Library of Congress, 6; PD, 6; Frank Leslie/Library of Congress, 7; National Library of Medicine/PD, 8; Irwin Gooen/Everett Collection/Alamy, 9; Ye Pingfan/Xinhua/Alamy, 10; Xinhua News agency/PD, 11; Meantea/CC3.0, 11; Everett Historical/Shutterstock.com, 12; Everett Historical/Shutterstock.com, 13; PD, 14; Joelwnelson/CC3.0, 15; Mary Noble Ours/NIDA(NIH)/PD, 16; NIDA(NIH)/PD, 17; Nora Volkow and Heinrich Schelbert/PD, 17; PD, 18; Cari Rubin Photography/Shutterstock.com, 19; Brian Katt/CC2.5, 19; National Institutes of Health/PD, 20; Samuel King Jr./US Air Force, 21; PD, 22-24; Francis Frith/PD, 25; ContentEditor949/CC3.0, 26; PD, 27; National Library of Medicine/PD, 28; Wellcome Collection/CC4.0, 29

ISBN
9781632357793 (hardcover)
9781632358882 (paperback)
9781645820598 (ebook)

Library of Congress Control Number: 2019938616

Printed in the United States of America
September 2019

About the Cover
Nora Volkow in 2013.

Access free, up-to-date content on this topic plus a full digital version of this book. Scan the QR code on page 31 or use your school's login at 12StoryLibrary.com.

Table of Contents

1 Antonia Novello: Surgeon General and Health Care Advocate

Antonia Novello is the first woman and first Latinx to become US Surgeon General. She was born Antonia Coella in Puerto Rico in 1944. As a child, she had an illness. She needed surgery at a faraway hospital. Her parents could not afford it. Every summer, she had to stay in a local hospital for treatment. It wasn't until she was 20 that she had the surgery. She decided to become a doctor. She wanted to help children stay healthy.

Antonia Novello in 2009.

Novello went to medical school in Puerto Rico. Then she went to the University of Michigan to specialize in kidney disease. She chose this because her aunt died of kidney failure. Novello wanted to improve the organ donor list system. Next, she became a pediatrician. In 1978, she began public health work. Her focus was on children's health. She found ways to help children with AIDS. She also helped Congress write laws about organ transplants.

In 1990, President George H.W. Bush chose Novello for Surgeon General of the United States. Novello worked for better health care for children, women, and minorities. She raised awareness about the dangers of underage

drinking. She spoke out against smoking, drug abuse, and AIDS. She promoted immunizations for children. She was an advocate for Latinx people and other minorities in need of health care.

THINK ABOUT IT

How did Antonia Novella respond to some of the hardships in her life? In what way did her problems inspire her to choose a career?

1993
Year when Antonia Novello became a UNICEF representative

- After leaving the Surgeon General post, she continued to work for health care for women, children, and minorities.
- She spoke out for good nutrition and substance abuse prevention.
- Novella received many awards, including the James Smithson Bicentennial Medal from the Smithsonian Institution.

2

Elizabeth Blackwell: First American Woman Doctor

Elizabeth Blackwell in 1877. She was commemorated on a US postage stamp in 1974.

Elizabeth Blackwell was the first woman to become a doctor in the United States. She was born in England in 1821. Her father was a sugar farmer. He was also a Quaker and an abolitionist. Blackwell had eight siblings. In 1832, the family moved to America. When Blackwell's father died in 1838, she went to work as a teacher.

One day, a dying friend told her she would have suffered less if her doctor had been a woman. Blackwell decided to become a doctor. She knew two male Quaker doctors. They helped her start to learn medicine. She applied to almost every medical school in the northeast United States. One school admitted her as a joke. The students and teachers treated her badly. But she persisted. In 1849, Blackwell became the first woman to get an MD degree from an American medical school.

Blackwell training women nurses at her infirmary.

Next, Blackwell worked in London and Paris hospitals. Although she had her degree, male doctors treated her like a nurse or midwife. She returned to New York in 1851 but could not find work because of her gender. She opened a clinic for poor women. In 1857, she and her sister Emily opened the New York Infirmary for Women and Children. Blackwell made a point of hiring women at the clinic. She also trained nurses. Blackwell founded the Woman's Medical College in New York City in 1868.

1st

Elizabeth Blackwell's class ranking when she graduated from medical school

- Blackwell hoped to become a surgeon, but an eye disease left her blind in one eye.
- She was a pioneer for women in medicine.
- Her younger sister, Emily, also became a doctor.

THINK ABOUT IT

Elizabeth Blackwell became a doctor at a time when only men were doctors. Can you think of any jobs today that are only for men? Or only for women?

3

Jane Cooke Wright: Cancer Treatment Pioneer

Jane Cooke Wright was an African American doctor and researcher. She changed how we treat cancer and has saved many lives. She was born in New York in 1919. Her father was one of the first black graduates of Harvard Medical School. He started the Cancer Research Center at Harlem Hospital. Wright graduated from medical college in 1946. In 1949, she began working with her father.

At the time, researchers were starting to try chemotherapy. This is the use of chemicals to treat cancer. Wright tested many chemicals to see which ones worked best. She came up with ways to treat cancer without surgery. She and her father tested a new chemical on patients with certain types of cancer. Several of the patients got better. When her father died in 1952, Wright became head of the Cancer Research Center. She was 33 years old.

In 1955, Wright became director of chemotherapy research at New York University Medical Center. President Lyndon B. Johnson named her to his President's Commission on Heart Disease, Cancer, and Stroke. Based on the commission's report, treatment centers were started across the country. In 1967, Wright became head of the Chemotherapy Department at New York Medical College. This made her the highest-ranking black woman at a major US medical institution.

Jane Cooke Wright in her cancer research lab in 1958.

1971

Year when Jane Cooke Wright became the first woman president of the New York Cancer Society

- Her career spanned 40 years.
- Her research advanced the use of chemicals to fight cancer.
- She traveled to Africa, China, Eastern Europe, and the Soviet Union to present her findings.

A FAMILY OF DOCTORS

Jane Cooke Wright's grandfather was born enslaved. After the Civil War, he got his medical degree. Wright's step-grandfather was the first black doctor to graduate from Yale. Wright's sister was a medical doctor as well.

4

Tu Youyou: Stamping Out Malaria

Tu Youyou with her medal following the Nobel Prize Award ceremony in 2015.

During the Vietnam War (1954–1975), Tu lead a group of scientists. Their goal was to find a cure for malaria. Many soldiers in the war had the disease. Many people in South Asia did, too. Tu studied plants used by Chinese healers. She developed an extract from a wormwood plant. It seemed to work against malaria. First, she used it on mice and monkeys. Then she tested it on herself to make sure it was safe for humans. She reported her findings to the World Health Organization (WHO) in 1972. Doctors began to use the extract to treat malaria.

In 2015, Tu won the Nobel Prize in Medicine. She shared the prize with two other scientists. The prize honors Tu for saving millions of lives. It praises her for combining traditional medicine with modern research. Tu's prize also honors scientific research in modern China.

Tu Youyou is the first Chinese woman to win a Nobel Prize. She was born in China in 1930. She studied at Beijing College and the China Academy. Her focus was on traditional Chinese medicine and modern Western drugs.

Tu doing research on wormwood with her tutor in the 1950s.

2,000+

Number of years wormwood was used in China to treat fevers

- Malaria is a serious disease spread to humans by mosquitoes.
- People with malaria suffer from flu-like symptoms and fever.
- If malaria isn't treated, it can lead to severe illness and death.

STRANGE COINCIDENCE

In Chinese names, the last name comes first. Tu's father got the name Youyou from a famous Chinese poem. In the poem, a deer makes a "youyou" sound while eating an artemisia plant. It is a strange coincidence that artemisia is the scientific name for the wormwood plant. Wormwood is the source of the extract used to treat malaria.

5

Florence Nightingale: The Lady with the Lamp

Florence Nightingale circa 1880.

Florence Nightingale paved the way for modern nursing. She was born to wealthy British parents in Florence, Italy, in 1820. Nightingale's father home schooled her. She was good at math as well as languages and history. At the time, young women were expected to become wives, mothers, and housekeepers. Nightingale wanted to learn nursing.

Nurses at the time were poor, unskilled workers. They worked in hospitals where sick people went to die. The hospitals were not kept clean. Nightingale's family told her nursing was not a respectable job. But she did not listen. She went to Germany in 1851 to learn to be a nurse. A Lutheran pastor there was working to make nursing better. In 1853, she got more training at a Catholic school in France. Then she took a job as head of a women's hospital in London.

In 1854, Nightingale led a group of 38 British nurses. They went to help at a hospital in Turkey. Hundreds of British soldiers were there for the Crimean War (1853–1856). Nightingale saw that the hospital needed change. Soldiers were not being given good food or medicine.

They slept in crowded, filthy rooms. They had no blankets. Many of the men had diseases caused by these conditions. More men were dying from diseases than from war injuries.

Nightingale and her team cleaned up the hospital. They gave the men nutritious food. They helped them write letters to their loved ones. At night, Nightingale walked around to check on the men. They called her the Lady with the Lamp.

1907

Year when Florence Nightingale was given the Order of Merit

- This is one of Britain's highest honors. Nightingale was the first woman to receive it.
- Nightingale wrote many books about nursing.
- She was known for her intelligence, determination, and hard work.

Nightingale's efforts during the Crimean War saved many soldiers.

6 Susan La Flesche Picotte: First Native American Physician

Susan La Flesche Picotte was the first Native American to become a medical doctor in the United States. She was born Susan La Flesche in 1865 on the Omaha Reservation in Nebraska. Her father was the chief of the reservation. He made sure his children got an education. He taught them to become leaders in their communities. When La Flesche was a child, a sick woman on her reservation died because the white doctor would not treat her. This inspired La Flesche to become a doctor.

Susan La Flesche Picotte circa 1900.

First, she became a teacher at the Quaker Mission School on the reservation. In 1886, she entered the Women's Medical College of Pennsylvania. She graduated one year early at the top of her class in 1889.

Then she went home to the reservation. La Flesche was the only physician, caring for over a thousand people. At the time, alcoholism and tuberculosis were big problems on the reservation. She worked to educate the

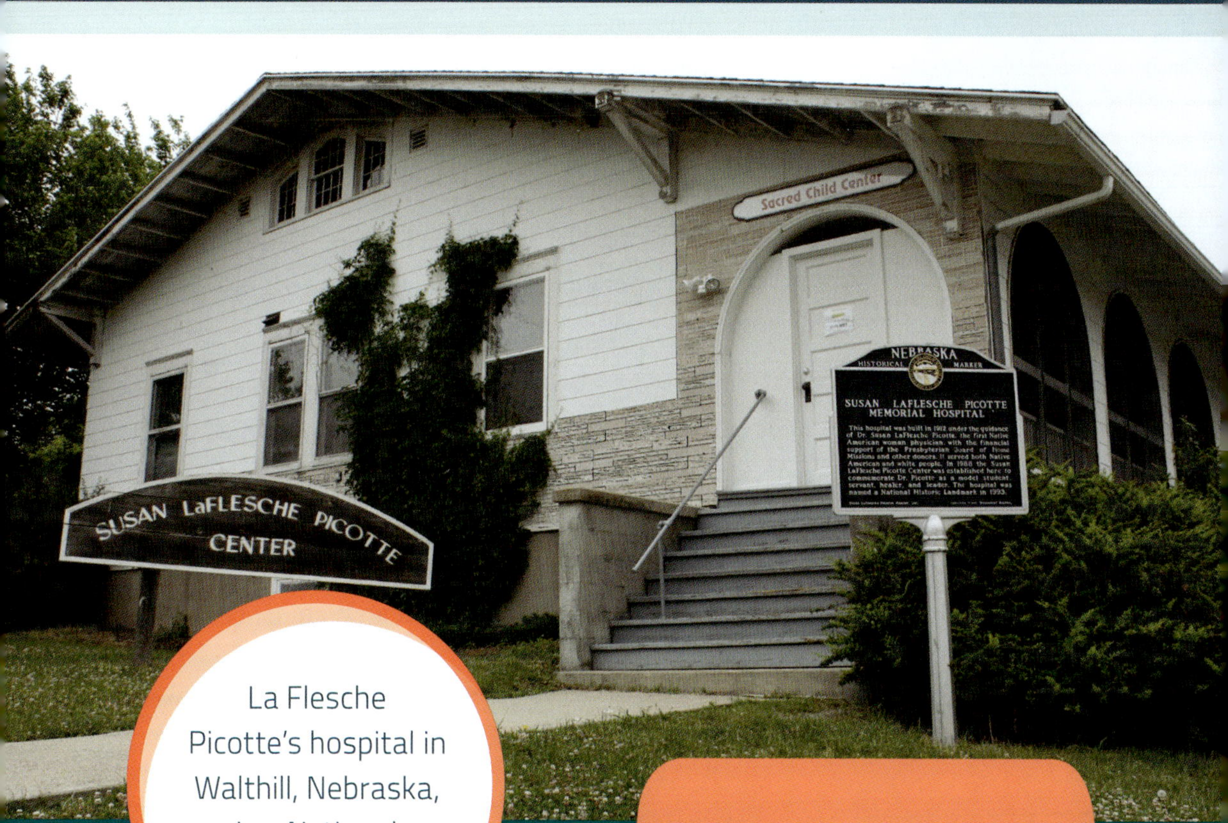

La Flesche Picotte's hospital in Walthill, Nebraska, is a National Historic Landmark.

people about prevention. She asked for help from the government.

In 1894, La Flesche married Henry Picotte. They had two sons. She continued to work as a doctor. In 1906, she led a group to Washington, DC. They fought to ban alcohol from the reservation. In 1913, she opened a hospital in Walthill, Nebraska. In 1993, the building was registered as a National Historic Landmark.

450

Size in square miles (1,165 sq km) of the reservation where Susan La Flesche Picotte was the only doctor

- La Flesche Picotte was the first person to get federal aid for college.
- She was the first Native American to receive a medical degree.
- She gave health care, financial advice, and counseling to the Omaha people.

7

Nora Volkow: Addiction Is a Brain Disease

Nora Volkow is head of the National Institute on Drug Abuse (NIDA). Her research has changed the way scientists and doctors view addiction. Volkow was born in Mexico City in 1956. She graduated from the National University of Mexico. She studied psychiatry at New York University.

Volkow scanned the brains of people addicted to drugs. She found that addiction is caused by changes in the brain. When someone uses a painkiller, for example, the brain makes more of a chemical called dopamine. Waves of dopamine rush to the brain's pleasure center. This makes the person feel good. But over time, the brain makes less dopamine. Then the person needs even more drugs to feel good.

Before Volkow's research, many doctors thought drug abuse was a sign of weakness. Often, they did not treat addicts with the same sympathy as people with other illnesses. Insurance companies did not pay for treatment. Because of Volkow's work, addiction is now seen as a brain disease. In 2008, Congress passed a new law. It requires insurance companies to pay for medical treatment for addiction.

Nora Volkow in 2013.

680+

Medical articles written by Nora Volkow

- She has written more than 100 book chapters and manuscripts.
- Volkow has also done important work in the areas of obesity, ADHD, and aging.
- *Fortune* magazine named her one of "34 Leaders Who Are Changing Health Care."

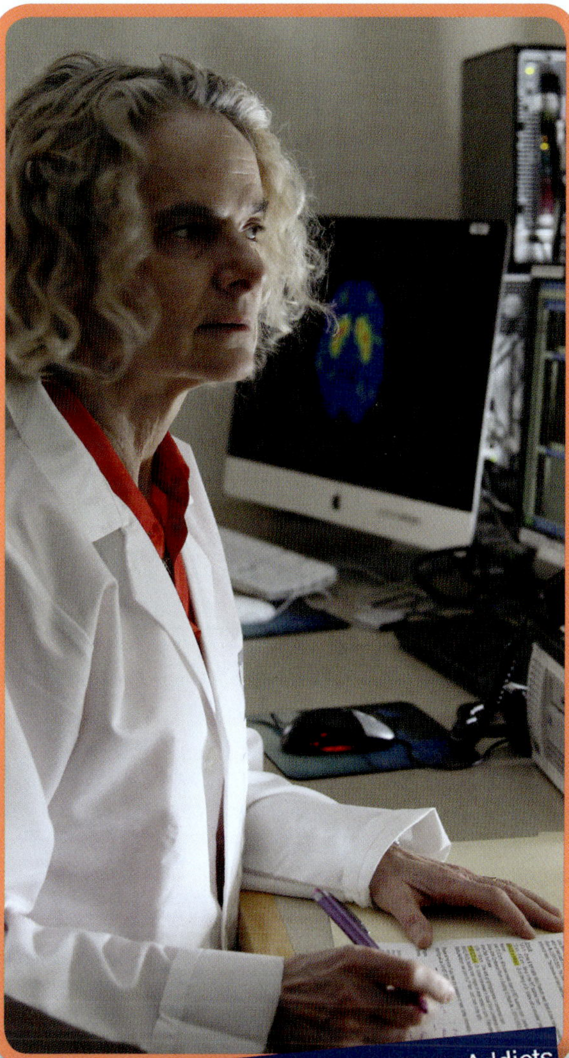

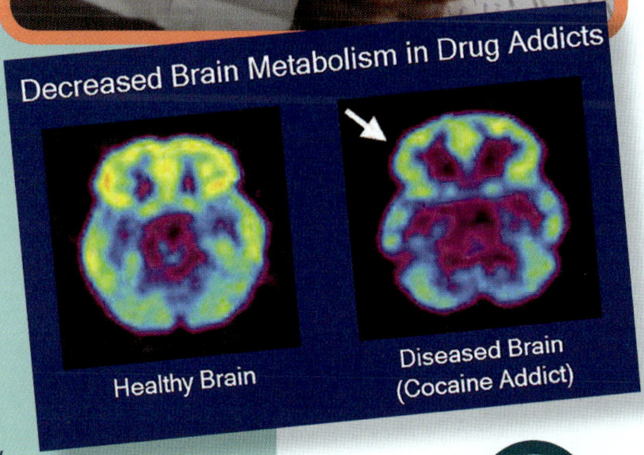

NORA VOLKOW'S GREAT-GRANDFATHER

Volkow's great-grandfather was Leon Trotsky. Born in 1879, he was a Russian revolutionary. He was forced to leave Russia for challenging the leaders in power. He escaped to Mexico City. He was assassinated there in 1940. Volkow grew up in the house where her great-grandfather was killed. She says she learned from her family history the importance of helping others.

8

Audrey Evans: Caring for Children with Cancer

Audrey Evans is a children's cancer specialist. She cofounded Ronald McDonald House Charities. Born in England in 1925, Evans knew by the time she was five that she wanted to be a doctor. She went to medical school in Scotland. Then she studied at Boston's Children's Hospital. From 1968 to 1989, she was head of the cancer center at Children's Hospital of Philadelphia (CHOP).

Evans was a pioneer in the study of treatment for childhood cancer. In 1971, she developed what is called the Evans Staging System. Doctors use it to find the best way to treat a certain kind of childhood cancer. It has enabled doctors to help 50 percent more children with this cancer to survive. Along with treating her patients' illness, Evans worked to ease their fears. She let them bring their pets to the hospital. She sat with them. She brought them their favorite foods.

Evans wanted to help the families of her patients, too. Many could not afford hotels. They slept in waiting room chairs and ate dinner from the hospital vending machines. In

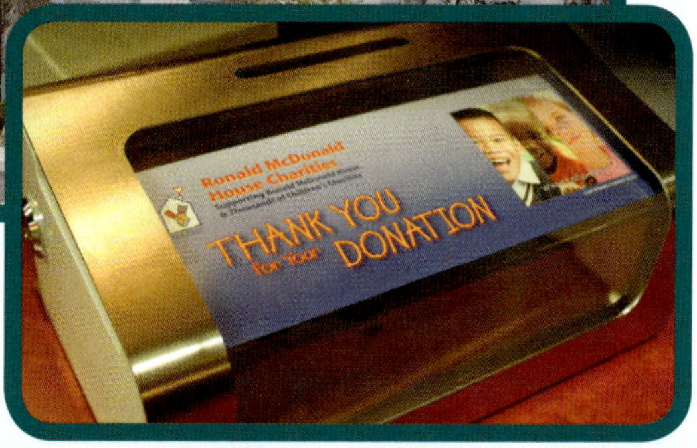

There are 360 Ronald McDonald Houses in the world today.

1974, she cofounded the first Ronald McDonald House in Philadelphia. This was a place where families could stay for free. They could have hot meals. They could be comfortable. And they could spend time with their children in the hospital.

Evans retired from CHOP in 2009. But she missed the children and wanted something to do. So she cofounded St. James School. It helps middle school students in Philadelphia who are at risk for poverty.

7 million

Number of families helped by Ronald McDonald House Charities

- There are Ronald McDonald Houses in more than 63 countries.
- They have 360 locations.
- The other cofounder was James Murray, a former general manager of the Philadelphia Eagles football team.

9

Patricia Bath: Leading the Fight against Blindness

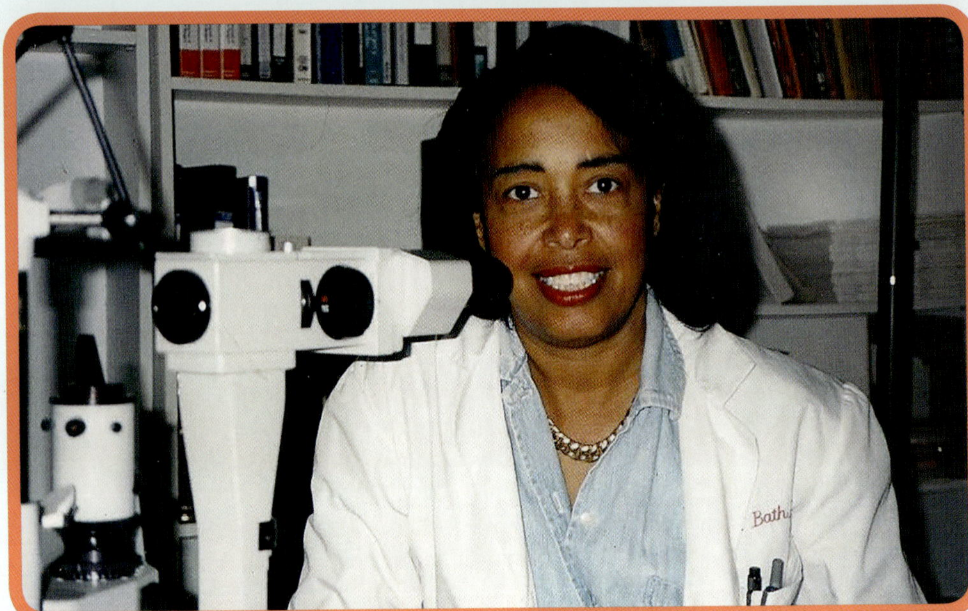

Patricia Bath is a champion in the treatment of blindness. She was born in Harlem, New York, in 1942. Her parents helped her get a good education. She loved science. At age 16, she wrote a math equation to predict the growth of cancer cells. She graduated from Howard University College of Medicine in Washington, DC, in 1968.

Bath worked at a clinic in Harlem. She noticed a puzzling difference between white patients and African American patients. The African Americans were twice as likely to be blind. Bath did a study to find the cause. She learned that African Americans needed better access to good eye care. She started a new field in medicine called Community Ophthalmology. This is an eye care program for underserved populations.

1976

Year when Patricia Bath co-founded the American Institute for the Prevention of Blindness (AIPB)

- The AIPB provides eye care for anyone, regardless of race, gender, age, or income.
- Bath was the first African-American female doctor to get a medical patent.
- She holds four US patents.

THINK ABOUT IT

Patricia Bath is a role model for women and for African Americans in medicine. Why are role models important? Which careers need more women or African American role models?

In 1973, Bath became the first African American to complete a residency in ophthalmology. In 1975, she became the first African American woman surgeon at the University of California, Los Angeles (UCLA) Medical Center. She was the first woman professor at the UCLA Eye Institute.

In 1981, Bath invented the laserphaco probe. This is a tool used to remove cataracts. Cataracts are cloudy areas that grow over the lens of an eye. People over age 60 often get them. If not removed, they can cause blindness. Bath's tool helps surgeons remove them safely and quickly.

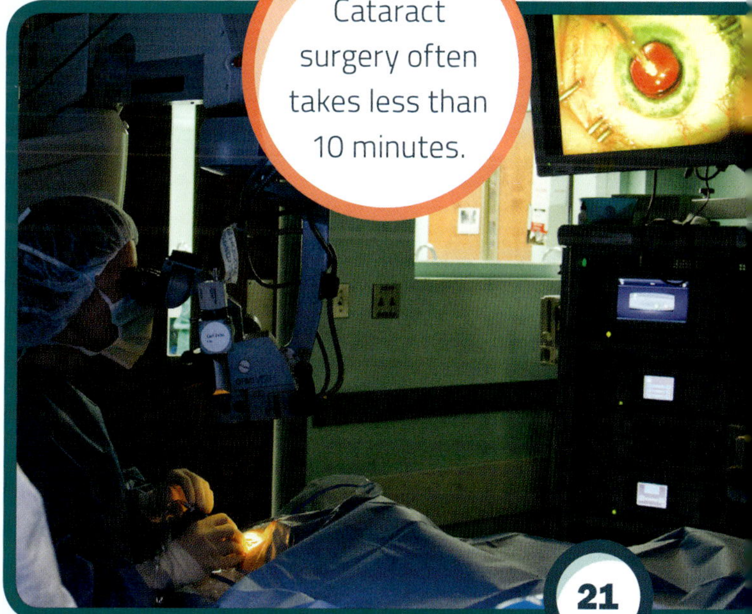

Cataract surgery often takes less than 10 minutes.

10

Helen Mayo: Health Crusader for Women and Children

Helen Mayo in 1914.

Helen Mary Mayo was an Australian doctor who worked to improve health for mothers and children. She was born in Adelaide, South Australia, in 1878. In 1898, she began to study medicine at the University of Adelaide. She was its second female medical graduate. For four years, she worked with mothers and infants in London, Dublin, and Delhi.

In 1906, Mayo returned to Adelaide. She worked as a midwife. She treated women and children. In 1911, she set up a vaccine department at the children's hospital. At the time, one in 12 infants in Australia died before they were a year old. Mayo wanted to help more babies survive. She started the Adelaide School for Mothers to teach mothers how to care for their babies. The school later grew into the Mothers' and Babies' Health Association.

In 1913, Mayo opened a hospital for babies. She showed mothers and doctors the best way to feed babies. She taught them how to prevent infection.

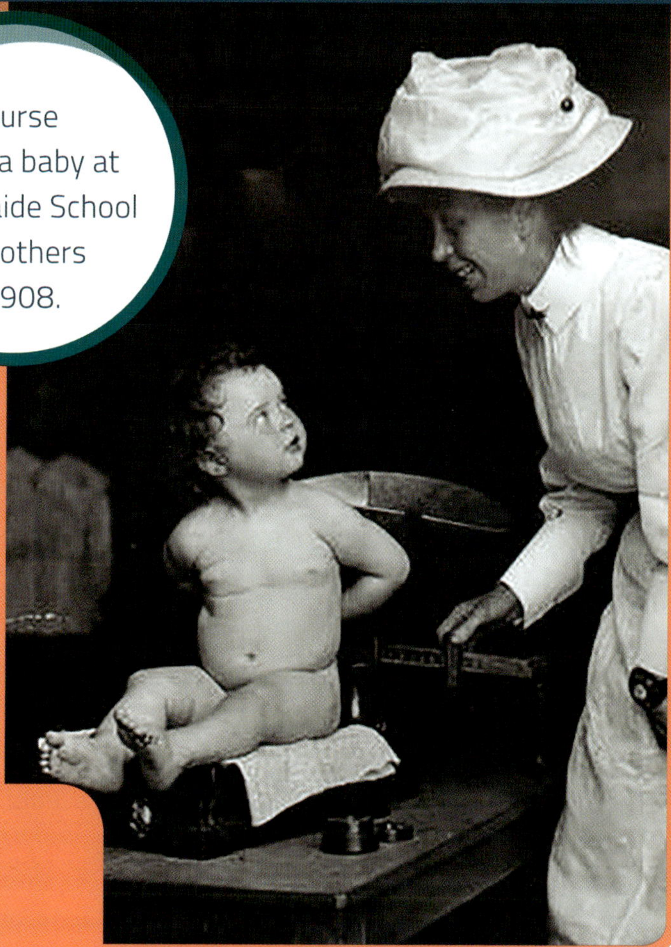

A nurse weighs a baby at the Adelaide School for Mothers in 1908.

Mayo was also an advocate for women's rights. She helped start St. Ann's University College for Women. She founded a women's political group. She was president of a club for career women and female artists.

60 percent

How much the infant death rate in South Australia fell during Helen Mayo's 40-year career

- Most of the other leaders in medicine were men.
- Before Mayo started medical school, she studied art. Her father thought she was too young to study medicine.
- Her hobbies included sketching and embroidery.

BACK TO WORK

Helen Mayo retired from medicine in 1938. When World War II broke out, she returned to the hospital. She worked there until the war ended. She was the head children's doctor. She set up the Red Cross blood donor system. She continued to teach about infant feeding.

11

Kadambini Ganguly: First Indian Woman Doctor

Kadambini Ganguly was the first Indian woman to become a doctor of Western medicine. She was born Kadambini Bose in India in 1861. Her father was from Bangladesh. He was a school headmaster and an advocate for women's rights. He sent Kadambini to a school in Calcutta, where she studied math and science as well as other subjects. At the time, most girls in India weren't allowed to go to school.

Dwarakanath Ganguly was one of the founders of the Calcutta school. He was also for women's rights. He helped Kadambini apply to the University of Calcutta. In 1878, she became the first woman to pass the University's entrance exam. In 1882, she was one of its first two women graduates. She decided to stay in school and study medicine.

In 1883, Kadambini and Dwarakanath were married. She

ROLE MODEL

Kadambini Ganguly worked as a doctor of women's health. She often delivered babies. She became well-known and popular. The Queen of England sent her a pony as a gift. She gained the attention of Florence Nightingale. Women in India saw her as a role model.

was 21 years old. He was 39. His first wife had died, and he had three children. Most women in India didn't have careers, especially after they married. But Kadambini's husband was in favor of her school and work. She graduated from Calcutta Medical College in 1886. She was the first Indian woman doctor of the British Indian Empire.

5

Number of children born to Kadambini and Dwarakanath Ganguly, bringing their total to eight

- Kadambini's career as women's health doctor spanned more than 30 years.
- Back then, women doctors were very rare.
- She paved the way for career women in India.

The University of Calcutta at the time Ganguly attended.

12

Susan Love: Working to End Breast Cancer

Susan Love is a doctor who wants to end breast cancer. She was born in New Jersey in 1948. Love graduated from medical school in 1974. At the time, only 10 percent of medical students were women. She was one of five who were at the top of their class.

Susan Love in 2013.

Love began to treat patients with breast cancer. She was an advocate for her patients. In 1990, she wrote a book for women with breast cancer. It helps them understand the disease and make choices about their treatment. Love also helped start the National Breast Cancer Coalition. This group got the US government to give more money for cancer research.

Love is president of the Dr. Susan Love Research Foundation. She is a professor of surgery at the University of California, Los Angeles (UCLA). Love raises awareness for patients who are having cancer treatment. She hopes to find the cause of breast cancer. She wants to stop cancer before it needs to be treated.

Love's book continues to be revised and updated since first published in 1990.

6

Number of years Susan Love served on President Bill Clinton's National Cancer Advisory Board

- *Dr. Susan Love's Breast Book* has been called the bible for women with breast cancer.
- Love helped start the Army of Women. This group helps scientists find volunteers for their research studies. It has more than 383,000 members.
- She helped develop an iPhone app to track the effects of treatment.

CANCER SURVIVOR

In 2012, Love found out she had leukemia. This is a cancer of the bone marrow. She had chemotherapy. Love is in remission now. She says the experience helped her understand how it feels to be a cancer patient. It also made her want to work faster to find a cure.

Out of the Shadows

Metrodora

Metrodora was a Greek doctor who lived sometime between 200-400 CE. She wrote the oldest known medical textbook by a woman. At the time, women usually helped with childbirth and women's health. Metrodora's book was about other areas of medicine as well.

Rosalyn Sussman Yalow

Rosalyn Sussman Yalow was born in 1921. She was the second woman to win a Nobel Prize in Medicine. She helped develop a way to detect diseases by measuring substances in the body. Because of her work, many illnesses can be found and treated.

Rosalyn Sussman Yalow.

A pen and ink drawing of Trotula.

Trotula

Trotula was an eleventh-century Italian doctor. She is known as Trotula of Salerno. She is often called the world's first gynecologist, or women's health specialist. She introduced the use of painkillers for childbirth. Doctors used the book she wrote about women's health for many years after her death in 1097.

Rebecca Lee Crumpler

Born in 1831, Rebecca Lee Crumpler was the first African American woman to earn a medical degree. She wrote the first medical book by an African American. She was inspired to go into medicine by her aunt, who often helped care for sick neighbors. She tended to freed slaves after the Civil War.

Glossary

abolitionist
A person who wants to stop slavery.

ADHD
ADHD stands for Attention Deficit Hyperactivity Disorder. This is a condition that makes it difficult for children to control their behavior.

AIDS
AIDS stands for Acquired Immunodeficiency Syndrome. This is a serious illness caused by a virus.

chemotherapy
The use of chemicals to treat diseases such as cancer.

ophthalmology
The branch of medicine that studies and treats eye disease.

pediatrician
A doctor who treats children.

psychiatry
The branch of medicine that studies and treats mental illness.

remission
The temporary recovery from a disease.

resident
A medical graduate student who practices under a supervisor in a hospital.

scan
To pass a special beam over a part of the body to make an image.

Read More

Gagne, Tammy. *Women in Medicine*. Women in STEM. Mankato, MN: ABDO Core Library, 2017.

Dickmann, Nancy. *Women Scientists in Medicine*. Superwomen in STEM. New York: Gareth Stevens, 2018.

Cooke, Tim. *Florence Nightingale*. Meet the Greats. New York: Gareth Stevens, 2017.

Index

About the Author

Marne Ventura has written over 100 books for children. A former elementary school teacher, she holds a master's degree in education from the University of California. Marne and her husband live on the central coast of California.